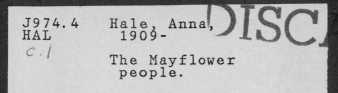

The
Mayflower People

The Mayflower People

TRIUMPHS & TRAGEDIES

by
Anna W. Hale

Illustrations by
Maria Hazen-Voris

· Harbinger House ·

TUCSON

• •

Harbinger House appreciates the cooperation and helpful guidance from the research department of Plimouth Plantation in the preparation of this book.

• •

Copyright © 1995 by Anna W. Hale

Illustrations © copyright by Harbinger House

Harbinger House
P.O. Box 42948
Tucson, AZ 85733-2948

Manufactured in the United States of America
Design, production and maps by Page by Page Studio
Cover illustration by Betsy Hall Hutchinson

10 9 8 7 6 5 4 3 2 1

Library of Congress Cataloging-in-Publication Data

Hale, Anna, 1909–
    The Mayflower people: triumphs and tragedies/Anna W. Hale;
illustrations by Maria Hazen-Voris.
        p. cm.
    Includes bibliographical references and index.
    Summary: Recreates the voyage of the Mayflower and the experiences
of the New Plymouth colonists after they landed, based on journals,
letters, and other contemporary reports.
    ISBN 1-57140-002-8. (hc)—ISBN 1-57140-003-6 (pbk)
    1. Mayflower (Ship)—Juvenile literature.   2. Pilgrims (New
Plymouth Colony)—Juvenile literature.   3. Massachusetts—History—
New Plymouth, 1620-1691—Juvenile literature.   [1. Mayflower
(Ship)   2. Pilgrims (New Plymouth Colony)   3. Massachusetts—
History—New Plymouth, 1620-1691.]   I. Hazen-Voris, Maria, ill.
II. Title.
F68.H135 1995   95-17355
974.4'8202—dc20

Contents

Author's Notes

Dates in this story are "Old Style," as used by the English at the time of the Pilgrims. When the Gregorian calendar was introduced in 1582, December 10 changed to December 21.

This story is about real people and real events as described in letters, records and other historical documents. Dialogue has been added to bring the story to life.

No one really knows the precise size and shape of the original Mayflower, but one clue is found in the writings of William Bradford, who mentions that she was a vessel of 180 tons. From this information historians and ship builders have estimated the following (approximate) measurements:
- Length of keel-64 feet
- Width (beam)-26 feet
- Depth of hold-11 feet

The original version of the Mayflower Compact has been adapted from the Old English to express its essential statement for today's readers.

Chapter 1

Takeoff—At Last!

On August 6, 1620, Master Jones of the Mayflower gave orders to hoist anchors and set the sails. Master Reynolds on the much smaller Speedwell did the same. Turning out of the harbor at Southampton, England, the two ships headed for the distant Atlantic.

These ocean going ships carried unusual cargo. They were loaded with fathers and mothers and children and all their household goods.

For three long years these people had planned, prayed, and prepared to settle in the New World. In America the king could not put them in prison—or kill their leaders—for separating from the Church of England, of which he was the head.

Also on board were a few people who were not Separatists. These were the Adventurers, who had paid to take part in the expedition in hope of finding gold.

In the cargo area were the usual supplies, as well as

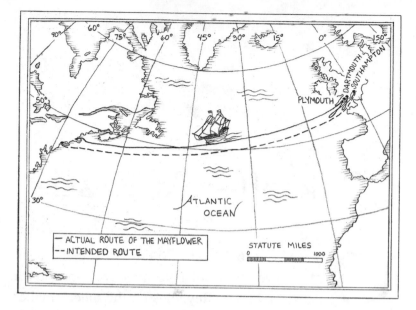

three heavy cannons for defense. Packed in sections was an
open boat called a "shallop," useful for exploring and fishing. The people had tried to think of everything they could
possibly need.

On the deck of the Mayflower stood Mary Brewster,
who had come from Holland with her sons Love, 9, and
Wrastle, 6. Her husband, Elder William Brewster, was the
leader of the group. He had been in England for some
months to make final arrangements, working under cover
because the king had ordered his arrest as a traitor.

Wrastle, looking worried, tugged at his mother's arm.

"Mother," he said, "Father *promised* to meet us here.
Where is he?"

"There's no way he can catch up with us now we are
moving," Love said.

8

Mary Brewster hugged and hushed her boys. "I don't know," she said. "But don't worry. We'll be all right."

She glanced across the deck at William Bradford and his wife, Dorothy, grateful they were there. Even before the Separatists had fled to Holland for safety, young Bradford had been Brewster's right-hand man. Mary respected and liked him although, at 31, he lacked the care for others that made her husband so trusted. She felt sorry for Dorothy, 23, who had to leave her only child—a boy of 4—behind with friends, because he was so often sick. Since parting from him she had hardly said a word to anyone. It was as though she had left her heart behind and nothing else mattered.

Mary Brewster understood. She had left children behind also, but they were teenagers, and they were to join the settlement next year if all went well.

Just before sailing, the Separatists and other passengers had chosen a senior man, John Carver, to be their governor for the voyage. And at the last minute, one more passenger had come aboard. This man, John Alden, was not a Separatist. He was a footloose young carpenter and barrel-maker who had been hired to take care of the countless barrels of food and other supplies in the hold of the Mayflower. It is possible, perhaps likely, that he had also caught a glimpse of Priscilla Mullins, one of the teenage girls on board.

The ships began to pick up speed. It was an exciting but scary moment. Now there could be no turning back. The Separatists were now *Pilgrims*, torn between their hope for freedom to worship God in their own way, and fear of the unknown wilderness where the native people might be unfriendly.

Others on board were probably thinking of how they would spend the gold they hoped to find in the New World.

On the deck near Mary Brewster and her sons were Stephen and Elizabeth Hopkins with their three children, and another on the way. These five would occupy one of the four tiny cabins on the Mayflower. Elizabeth whispered to her husband.

"Stephen, are you sure we'll get settled before the baby comes?"

Of course," he answered quickly. "In good summer weather the crossing will take six, maybe seven weeks. Say to the end of September. We'll have houses built long before the end of November."

"I hope so," she said.

Next to them stood William Mullins and his wife, from the English town of Dorking. With them was their son Joseph, 6, and their daughter Priscilla, an attractive 18-year-old. She had not wanted to leave her home and friends. It is easy to imagine that she had already made plans for her future—plans that would not come true if she crossed the Atlantic. She had begged to stay with her grandparents, but her stubborn father refused. He wanted all of them to take part in the new settlement.

Also watching the ships' progress were Captain Miles Standish and his wife, Rose. This short, stocky soldier with bristling red hair and beard was responsible for the military protection of the Pilgrim colony. He had combat experience and a voice like a drill sergeant. He intended to use the weeks at sea to train the men for military action. The Separatists and the other men needed to be able to understand and obey his commands. They also needed to be able to shoot straight. Rose Standish, even shorter than her husband, was as quiet as he was blustery.

When darkness fell that first night and everyone was below, the Separatists were very upset. Elder Brewster, their leader, had not shown up.

"Why didn't he come on board in Southampton as planned?" they asked each other.

No one answered that question.

"Do you suppose he was arrested by the king's soldiers at the last minute?"

There was a pause before someone said, "We don't know. But we do know there's no way he can join us now."

That night it was hard for many Pilgrims to sleep. They knew they could not get along without Brewster's wisdom, courage, and leadership.

| August 7 | The next morning, as the families gathered in the main cabin, everyone stared with surprise. They could not believe their eyes. There stood Elder Brewster with Mary and the boys, greeting everyone with a warm smile and open arms!

"How did you get here?" they demanded.

Brewster's eyes twinkled. "I came on board very quietly one night in Southampton," he said. "Since then I have been hidden away and wonderfully cared for in a secret hideout!"

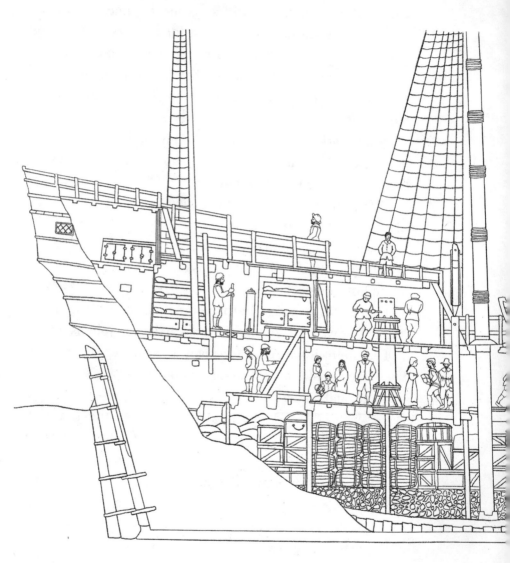

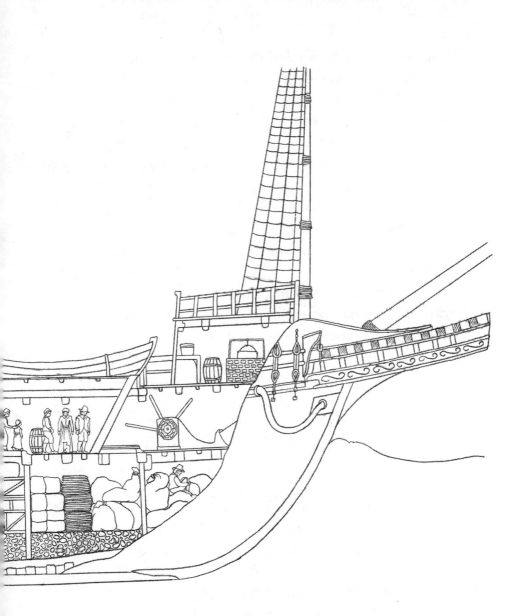

The amazed and grateful Pilgrims were sure now that all would go well, according to their careful plans.

| August 10 | But it was not to be. On the fifth day out of Southampton, having gone about 125 miles along the south coast of England, the Speedwell began to leak. Both ships had to go into Dartmouth harbor to get it repaired.

Master Jones was angry at this delay. He swore and shouted. "I *knew* rotten things would happen when the other three owners insisted on my taking a dirty cargo across the Atlantic!"

"What's a 'dirty cargo'?" someone asked.

It was the first mate who answered. "That's what sailors call it when a ship carries *people* instead of things!"

The repairs took several days. Then the Pilgrims faced another difficulty: finding the money to pay the repair bill and the harbor fees.

This was a need they had never imagined. What could they do? Finally someone said, "Maybe we can sell some of our casks of butter."

"No! We'll need that later!"

But that was what they had to do.

| August 16 | They made their second start on August 16. With a favoring wind they moved eastward again, and after a few days passed Land's End, the western tip of England. Almost everyone came on deck to catch a last glimpse of their homeland before it disappeared into the ocean behind them.

Captain Standish started to train his troops.

He lined them up and began to explain the commands. He soon learned the deck space on the tiny ship was not big enough for military maneuvers, especially as the ship kept heeling to the side. So, knowing that few of the men had ever handled a gun, he began to teach them to shoot.

Muskets were brought up from storage and handed out. Each man was also given a bag of lead pellets, called "shot," to tie at his waist, and a powder horn for gunpowder. The powder horn was to be slung over one shoulder.

Standish showed them how to pour gunpowder and shot into the gun barrel and shake gunpowder into the flash pan of the musket.

"You must learn to use a slow-match," he said. He handed each man a piece of string which had been soaked in a chemical called saltpeter. "Fasten this in the clip near the flash pan of your musket."

He went on, "Before we fight, one man in each group will light his match using flint and steel. Then the slow-burning flame will be passed from man to man."

They practiced those steps over and over again. Finally the captain said, "I will show you, once, how to set the gunpowder on fire with the match, while aiming my gun and pulling the trigger."

The men near him jumped a bit when the charge exploded.

Standish scowled. "We can't practice shooting while we're on the ship," he announced. "It would waste powder and shot." He sighed. "God only knows when we will ever get more."

The days passed slowly for the passengers. They were

cheered one day when Master Jones announced that they had come a good 300 miles beyond Land's End.

Not long after that, however, there came a shout from the lookout high in the rigging of the Mayflower.

"Master! Distress signal on the Speedwell!"

Jones ordered sails lowered to slow the ship. He signaled the other vessel to come alongside.

"What's wrong?" he bellowed.

"She's leaking again," Reynolds yelled. "Bad."

Jones thought quickly.

"Plymouth is your nearest harbor. That's not too far. You should be able to make it."

Reynolds called back. "I can't risk it with so many passengers. We're in danger of sinking even if we use the pumps night and day."

Brewster and others discussed the situation with Jones. Finally they decided both ships must turn around and sail back to Plymouth. If the Speedwell began to sink, the passengers and crew could be taken aboard the Mayflower.

The master was furious. This second delay seemed an insult. It cut across his plan for a quick crossing and his return to England before winter. And of course he blamed it on the Separatists. Why couldn't they stay where they belonged and worship in the king's church?

As they retraced the weary, watery miles some of the Pilgrims were asking themselves questions too. Were these troubles a sign they were on the wrong track?

Finally, with the smaller ship still afloat, they came into Plymouth harbor. Work was begun on the Speedwell. The passengers were glad to stretch their legs ashore and eat some fresh food. They found the people of Plymouth very friendly and hospitable. Some of them even invited the Pilgrims into their homes.

Before the Speedwell was ready, Master Reynolds went to talk with Jones and the Pilgrim leaders. "I will not take that rotten tub out into the Atlantic again," he announced.

Brewster was shocked into silence.

Jones demanded, "Why not?"

"She's not seaworthy. The new mast put in just before the voyage is too tall for the vessel. It will tear the hull apart, especially in storms."

Quietly Elder Brewster said, "Reynolds, we hired you and your crew for twelve months' service. This is a business venture as well as a venture of faith. Cushman, Weston, and other merchants have invested money in our project. In turn, we have agreed to send them, for seven years, all the New World products we can raise or get by trading.

"Your ship must stay with us until we load it with goods for you to take back to London. You'll also carry letters to the merchants and our friends with news of our progress.

"We further count on you and the Speedwell to bring back to us, before your year of service is over, more settlers and vital supplies."

After a long minute Reynolds said, "I will not go."

When nobody spoke, he added, "I'll tell you what I *will* do! I'll take back to London, free of charge, all who want to go!"

No matter how they argued, no matter what benefits they offered, Reynolds refused to change his mind.

Jones hoped the Separatists would accept this chance and give up their project. Some may have wanted to turn back. But the leaders never faltered, sure that a good future awaited them across the ocean. Such steadfastness puzzled as well as angered the Mayflower's master.

John Billington was not a Separatist. He had come from London's inner city with his wife and two young sons in search of wealth. He and his family often made fun of the Pilgrims' beliefs, but he too refused Reynold's offer. With a laugh he said, "I have faith too. I trust Master Jones' seamanship! I have faith in the sturdy Mayflower. We'll get to the New World all right."

With these decisions made, the Speedwell's passengers, about twenty-five people, had to move onto the Mayflower with all their possessions.

Once more Priscilla Mullins urged her parents to let her stay in England. Once more they refused. They felt their family was meant to play a vital role in the New World. So the teenager went up on deck to watch people moving their belongings from the Speedwell. She was puzzled when she saw men struggling to get a strange, heavy metal object off the Speedwell and into the longboat.

"What in the world is that?" she asked.

John Alden had come to stand beside her. "I think that's kind of metal screw," he said.

She was curious. "What is it for?"

"It is a tool carpenters use when building a house or

barn. With two or more men turning it, they can get a heavy beam into exactly the right spot where they want to fasten it."

"Oh, I see," Priscilla said. She nodded her head. "And of course we'll need it for building homes in our settlement."

"Not necessarily," Alden told her. "We can build small frame houses more quickly and easily if we don't use a house-screw."

| September 5 | On September 5, when the May-flower finally set sail again, the ship was dangerously overloaded. Now it carried 102 passengers—fifty men, twenty women, and thirty-two children and young people—as well as the master, two mates, and a crew of about twenty. All on a ship designed for no more than a handful of passengers.

By now the settlers were a month behind schedule. They still hoped to reach northern Virginia before autumn hurricanes threatened to make the Atlantic a deathtrap.

They scarcely dared to think beyond their arrival. What if winter weather came before they could build houses? What if the natives were fierce and warlike?

Brewster, Carver, and Bradford encouraged others by their own firm conviction that they would get safely to Virginia and build a permanent settlement. This hopeful outlook was strengthened by the favorable winds that hurried them along for almost three weeks. Even so, life on the crowded vessel grew more unpleasant every day.

The Pilgrim men, used to working long hours at their different trades, had nothing to do. The women always had

20

handwork to keep them occupied, but they were never free of the fear that their youngsters might fall overboard. When the children ran around on the decks, the sailors would yell at them to go below.

One sailor, Richard Salterne, took special delight in teasing the Pilgrims. He did not believe in God at all, and made fun of their faith. He would mimic them and say terrible things. "Your God plans to drown you in the ocean!" he would say. "Or let wild beasts or savages kill and eat you on land! I wouldn't trust Him to take care of me. I can take care of myself!"

They tried to ignore his taunts, but it was hard to keep quiet. He bothered them every chance he got.

The Billingtons, with their rough language and rude manners, were another trial. Mothers like Mary Brewster and Elizabeth Hopkins tried to be friendly but at the same time protect their children from bad habits.

Even mealtime was an ordeal. Shipboard food was dull and unappetizing, and day after day it was the same. For breakfast there was gruel, a watery cereal served hot the day it was cooked and cold the next two days. The other meal was dried or salted meat, with hard biscuits and no butter. It didn't help that Master Jones had a different menu, cooked just for him.

The smell below was sickening. Toilet facilities were primitive and washing was almost impossible. Fresh water was for drinking only, and was kept under lock and key. Passengers tried hauling up buckets of sea water to wash themselves.

"That won't do any good!" the sailors said, laughing at

them. "Salt water's no good for washing, so you'd better stop trying!"

Not everyone was idle, though. The three Pilgrim leaders and a few other committed men spent hours working together to plan for the thousand and one details they would face as soon as they landed.

Brewster and several other men and women made special efforts to help adults and children pass the time happily and creatively. They shared their few books. They held Bible studies. They organized games and crafts and invented new ones. One or two good storytellers were on board; they could hold the attention of children and grownups alike.

The Adventurers, including the Billingtons, were welcome to join these activities. Sometimes they did. Only Dorothy Bradford, still missing her little son, seemed to prefer being by herself.

Near the end of September, fierce storms and hurricanes swept the North Atlantic, blowing the Mayflower far off course. Only Jones' skill and the strength of his crew kept the vessel afloat. Life on board became even more miserable and scary, especially for those who were seasick.

October Stephen Hopkins, knowing their baby was almost due, must have said to himself time and again, "We'd be on land by now if only we hadn't lost four whole weeks on account of the Speedwell."

Instead, not even Jones knew exactly where on the wide Atlantic they were.

One night Richard Salterne began to complain of severe

pain in his right side. The man who acted as the ship's doctor could not help him. Neither could the Pilgrims' deacon, Dr. Sam Fuller. For three days and nights Salterne screamed in agony. Then he died, possibly of a ruptured appendix. He was buried at sea, with Master Jones conducting the ceremony.

Apparently Salterne's death shocked Jones because it had come so suddenly, so mysteriously, to the sailor who was cruelest to the Pilgrims.

November came and Elizabeth Hopkins gave birth to a baby boy. Because they were somewhere on the ocean, she named him Oceanus.

The storms continued. Then came the time when one enormous wave curved high over the Mayflower and landed with all its weight and force on the center of the ship.

The noise of the impact was deafening as water flooded into the living quarters on the lower decks. It could not drown out another frightening sound: the cracking of the huge beam in the roof of the main cabin where people were huddled together in terror.

The ship was breaking up.

Almost before they caught their breath, the master and the ship's carpenter were there with lanterns, staring at the split beam. Jones demanded, "Chips, can you mend it?"

Chips studied the damaged. Then soberly he said, "I might be able to, if I had a house-screw to force the two parts of the split beam together."

"Well, get your house-screw!"

Almost angrily, the carpenter replied. "Sir, I never heard of a ship carrying a house-screw!"

No one spoke, as they took in this fact.

Elder Brewster had made his way through the crowd to stand beside Jones. "What do we do next, sir?" he asked.

Jones scowled. "There's only one thing we can do," he barked. "Throw the cargo overboard. First of all your heavy cannons."

Captain Standish burst out angrily. "Absolutely not, sir!" he said. "We need those cannons."

Elder Brewster protested also. "That's impossible! If we lose our equipment, we cannot build our town."

Furious, Jones growled, "Mr. Brewster, if we don't lighten the ship as much as we possibly can, we'll all drown. You won't have to worry about making a settlement."

John Alden spoke up. "When I checked the casks and barrels in the hold, I saw what I think is a house-screw. Shall we get it?"

No one knew for sure if it would work, but it was worth a try. Several men went down into the cargo hold and brought up the heavy metal screw.

With Chips directing them they piled wooden boxes on each other and then set the screw right under the split beam. Then two men wriggled into position to turn the arms of the screw.

People held their breath as they watched. The men strained every muscle, and slowly . . . slowly . . . the jagged piece of wood inched into place.

Then Chips took spare boards and began fastening them,

like splints on a broken bone, to the beam. He used plenty of long, strong nails.

That night there were prayers of praise and thanks from the Mayflower passengers and crew.

Master Jones could not help noticing the unbelievable fact that a house-screw—the one thing that could save the ship—was on board with the Separatists. He may not have said anything, but he began to think differently about them. First there had been Salterne's unexplained death, and now this. Who was he, Jones, to despise these people if they had the blessing of the Almighty?

The storms had done their worst. The crippled Mayflower moved toward the New World once more. Not many days later a cry came from the lookout.

| November 9 | Land! On the weather side!"
Everyone rushed onto deck. The ocean-sky horizon was broken for the first time since England had dropped out of sight. They saw no high hills, but definitely solid land.

The date was November 9. Later the master reported that he had tried to go further south but got into rough, shallow water. Because the ship was already badly damaged, he felt he had to turn back.

| November 10 | As he maneuvered the Mayflower inside the protecting arm of Cape Cod and dropped anchors, the Pilgrims shouted and rejoiced. They were worn out and some were sick, but they had reached the New World! They laughed and cried for joy.

Their joy did not last long. Master Jones called the lead-

ers together outside his cabin. He glared at them and declared: "I cannot and will not risk this ship by trying to go south to Virginia. You and your people will have to settle somewhere in this area."

He went on. "Put your shallop together. Explore this coast, and choose your site. While you do that, my sailors will repair the Mayflower. As soon as your goods are unloaded we will set sail for home while we still have enough food for the trip."

The master turned on his heel, went in the cabin, and closed the door.

The Pilgrims were stunned. There was dead silence. Had they survived the terrors of the Atlantic only to be dumped on this barren coast where they had no right to be?

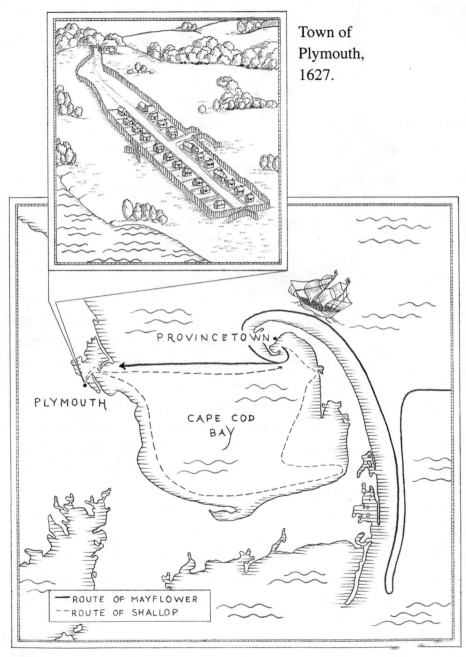

Town of Plymouth, 1627.

PROVINCETOWN

PLYMOUTH

CAPE COD BAY

ROUTE OF MAYFLOWER
ROUTE OF SHALLOP

Chapter 2

The Wrong Place

The leaders talked about what to do. An unexpected danger worried them.

In Virginia the settlers would have been under the accepted laws and regulations of the Virginia Company. Here, outside any recognized authority, it was possible the Adventurers might desert the colony to seek their own fortunes. Also, the Pilgrims from England and those from Holland did not always see eye to eye. Brewster and Carver felt it was important to weld the group into a single body, under rules accepted by all, before anyone set foot on shore.

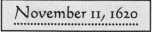

November 11, 1620 | Working together, they had soon written a short agreement later to be known as "The Mayflower Compact." It was the first American document to express the idea of government "of the people, by the people, for the people."

In the agreement the settlers pledged their allegiance to the King of England. It then continued: "We, whose names are signed here . . . having undertaken for the glory of God

and advancement of Christian faith . . . a Voyage to plant a colony . . . do solemnly, in the presence of God and each other, covenant and combine ourselves into a Civil Body Politic, for our better order and preservation . . . and to enact, constitute and frame such just and equal laws . . . acts, constitutions, and offices . . . as shall be most meet for the general good of the colony; unto which we promise all due submission and obedience. In witness whereof, we have hereunder subscribed our names. Cape Cod, eleventh of November, A.D. 1620."

It was a new idea for people to plan and carry out their own government. In 1620 even England did not have a written constitution.

The leaders signed first, then the other Separatist men, including John Alden. During the voyage Alden had studied with Elder Brewster and had joined the Pilgrim group. The young carpenter had also fallen in love with Priscilla Mullins and hoped to marry her. Some of the Adventurers signed the compact too; a few did not. Later, in the first election held in America, the signers chose John Carver as their governor for a one-year term.

While this history-making action was taking place on the ship, Master Jones was making a quick, official inspection of the land. With a dozen well-armed sailors, he was rowed to the nearby beach where he found only wind-whipped bushes, a few stunted trees, and driftwood blown ashore from other places.

Moving forward very cautiously, he saw no sign of native people. A world of wind and sand, it certainly could not support human life. However, he did find a marsh, fed by fresh-water springs, which would be useful. Returning to the ship, he said to the Pilgrim leaders, "You must build your shallop on this nearby sandspit, right away."

Alden and others went down into the hold to find and uncrate the sections of the fishing boat. Then these clumsy items had to be moved to the sandspit.

In the meantime Standish and several men were rowed to the main beach about a mile away. There, with awe, they stood for the first time on New World land. It was a dream come true, but it had turned into a nightmare. At their backs lay the forbidding Atlantic; before them were unknown dangers. As they staggered around on legs grown unsteady after months on board ship they saw a vast, empty land. They saw a few trees and acres of sand. This was not where they had planned to be.

What had gone wrong? What could they do?

With muskets ready and slow-matches burning, they walked a short distance on the beach, then climbed the low dunes and headed inland. They hoped to find friendly natives to trade with, yet they had to be prepared for attack. All they found was a discouraging repetition of bushes, scrawny trees, and more sand. How far would they have to go to find land for farms and gardens?

As darkness began to fall they trudged back to the beach. This was still November 11.

| November 12 | The next day Captain Standish again organized a group of Pilgrims for more exploring. Master Jones refused their request for the

longboat, so they had to plod at low tide over the wet sand. This time they headed for a point of land that rose about seventy feet above the sea. From the top they studied the strange shape of Cape Cod. There was no sign of human life except near their tiny anchored ship.

That morning Master Jones woke up in terrible pain from a bad tooth. He was like a wounded bear, dangerous and unreasonable. He sent for Giles Heale, the purser and sailmaker who served as the ship's doctor. Heale clamped a pair of carpenter's pliers around the tooth, but before he could pull it out, Jones punched him so hard he went reeling out of the cabin.

Five minutes later, Sam Fuller, the Pilgrim's doctor, knocked on the door, offering to help. Hopeless but hurting, Jones let him in.

Fuller knew how to handle a difficult patient. While Jones drank brandy to dull the pain, the doctor chatted about other things. He ignored the master's rude and crude remarks. Finally he persuaded Jones to let him add to his mug of brandy several drops of liquid from a tiny bottle he held.

"This medicine I got from the university in Holland is made of opium. If you drink just a bit," he promised, "I can pull out your tooth and you won't even know I'm doing it!"

"You're lying," the master said. But he let the doctor put a few drops into the brandy and drained the mug.

Before long Jones was unconscious. When he woke up, the tooth and the pain were both gone. He couldn't believe it, but there was the rotten tooth on the table near him.

Who and what were these Separatists? Such extraordinary things happened around them! The master was no longer bitter and critical. In fact, he was beginning to want to help them!

November 13 On Monday, November 13, it was judged safe to ferry the women and children to the near shore. After fourteen weeks cooped up in the ship, the youngster went wild, running and romping and tumbling on the beach. Their mothers were just as excited to learn that fresh water was available. They could hardly wait to bring kettles ashore, build fires to heat the fresh water, and wash clothes.

Dorothy Bradford alone showed no relief that the ocean trip was over. As she had borne the voyage without complaining she accepted the landing without joy. Her husband was so busy he scarcely noticed her unhappiness.

The Mayflower by now was an active community in a very small space. Under Carver's leadership the passengers were working to develop a cooperative self-government. The top priority was the building of their shallop. John Alden, the young carpenter, was in charge of the project, and other men handy with tools worked with him every daylight hour. Another group took turns standing guard on the deck of the Mayflower to protect the builders from

sudden attack. Still others tended fires to keep the carpenters' fingers from freezing.

Six people had become seriously ill, so a sick bay was established where they could be cared for by men and women who volunteered for nursing duty.

Other groups took on work details such as filling casks with fresh water from the springs near the marsh and cutting driftwood for the fires.

Master Jones was overseeing Chips and several sailors as they repaired the ship and reinforced the broken beam in the main cabin.

| November 15 |

On Wednesday, November 15, Captain Standish and fifteen Pilgrim men prepared for another exploring expedition. They planned to take enough food and equipment for two nights away from the ship. On deck they met Master Jones, who was about to go duck-hunting. The longboat was waiting to take him to the marsh.

When Jones saw the group he stopped short, frowning. A few days earlier he had refused point-blank to let his sailors take the Pilgrims to the spot where they wanted to begin their explorations. Now he tried to smile. "When the boat has taken me to the swamp," he said, "I'll tell the sailors to come back for you. Good luck!"

The Pilgrims were so surprised they barely managed to say, "Thank you, sir!"

They were grateful but puzzled. "Why, all of a sudden, is Master Jones acting so friendly?" they wondered.

Before the explorers set off, Governor Carver and

William Brewster reminded them of the rules that had been laid down for contact with native people.

"Remember, our purpose is to make friends, not enemies. You are not to shoot unless you have been attacked. Even then, aim not to kill but to frighten them. Let them know we are not like sailors from other ships, interested only in wealth and women."

After landing and arranging to make signal fires to communicate, they walked awhile on the shore, looking into the bushes where natives might be hiding. Suddenly one of the men looked ahead and shouted, "Look! People on the beach! And a dog!"

Eager to meet these strangers, they walked faster. However, by the time they reached that spot, the natives had disappeared into the sand hills.

It was easy to follow their tracks, but catching up with them was a different story. The natives could travel quickly, while the Englishmen were loaded down with supplies. Hour after hour they struggled on, stopping now and then for rest and food.

At last they came to a high ridge. Fearing an ambush, they spread out to climb it carefully. On reaching the top they gasped with surprise. They saw no natives, but below them lay the white breakers of the Atlantic Ocean, crashing on the outer shore of Cape Cod.

The natives had turned right, and their footprints were still clear, but the hour was late. The settlers decided to camp nearby. Some of them slept; others were too weary and sore to sleep.

In the morning, still hoping to find the natives' village, they followed the tracks for hours but without success. By afternoon, tired and disappointed by their failure, they headed for the inner shore of the Cape.

Stumbling along, guided by Captain Standish's compass, they found themselves walking in a field full of thick, cut-off stalks. A corn field! This was a real discovery—something to record on a map. Excited and encouraged, they searched the area carefully, and found not only the remains of a native home but two baskets full of corn.

The Pilgrims had heard about this New World grain and planned to buy some for seed. Here was their first chance to get some. Leaving the baskets, they bundled the corn in blankets and took it with them. They intended to pay for the corn as soon as they made contact with the native people.

When they returned to the Mayflower the next day, things on board were much the same as when they had left, though more people were ill. John Alden told them, "The shallop will be ready for the water in less than a week. And—can you believe it?—Jones himself has been working with us!"

Four days later the boat was launched and tied alongside the Mayflower. When the mast had been rigged and the rudder and leeboards put in place, Alden and three sailors hired to help the Pilgrims for a year climbed aboard. They practiced sailing the boat back and forth until they knew how to manage it. Designed for inland waters, the shallop was a wide, awkward craft with no deck.

"Never mind," one sailor said. "In high winds we can drop the sails and use the oars."

| November 21 | Soon the boat was ready for a trial run along the coast, but to everyone's disgust the weather changed. For three days wind, rain, sleet, and snow kept them aboard the Mayflower.

By noon on Sunday the weather had cleared, though it was still cold. They prepared to sail to Corn Hill the next day. Master Jones was eager to go with them, along with a few of his sailors, so when they set out on Monday morning thirty-four men were crowded into the shallop.

| November 27 | All went well. Landing at a place they named Cold Harbor, they shot three wild geese and six ducks and built a fire to roast the birds. For the first time since early September the men feasted on fresh meat. After their meal they searched the area thoroughly, finding more corn but no native people. They now had ten bushels of dried corn.

| November 28 | One night of camping was enough for Jones, so the shallop took him, and Pilgrims who had fallen ill, back to the Mayflower. The others stayed, still hoping to contact some of the people

they called "Indians" because of a mistake Columbus had made 128 years earlier. When he landed in the New World he thought he had reached India.

They were disappointed, but did find two native dwellings which had been used recently. Inside were not only woven baskets but bowls made of clay. It was clear that human beings did live in the area. But what kind of people were they? Wild and warlike, or reasonable and friendly? These questions were still unanswered when the shallop came to pick them up.

Brewster, Bradford, Carver, and other leaders decided it was time to forget the nearby natives and concentrate on finding a suitable location for their settlement. Provisions and equipment for a week or more were stowed away on the shallop and they planned to leave the following day.

| December 6 |

But four more days of bitter cold and windstorms closed in on them. At last, on Wednesday, December 6, in spite of the freezing temperatures, they set off. To help with navigation, Jones sent with them Clarke and Coppin, his first and second mates. Altogether there were twelve men on board, including all the Pilgrim leaders except Brewster.

Watching from the deck of the Mayflower, their wives must have thought, "If anything happens to that little boat, we are all lost!"

| December 7 |

After sailing about twenty miles the explorers saw in the distance a small group of natives on the shore, cutting up what they thought was a big fish. By the time the shallop had beached nearby, the natives—who had been butchering what was actually a small whale—had run so fast and far that the Pilgrims could not find them.

| December 8 |

Night came. The men camped ashore, alert for an attack. Eager to continue exploring, they were up again before dawn. They were eating breakfast when yells and shrieks burst from the scrawny trees at the top of the beach. Standish and a couple of other men fired their muskets in that direction without making a hit. A small flight of arrows from the unseen enemy did no harm, but the hair-raising yells grew louder.

One settler put birdshot in his musket and fired above the heads of the natives. Leaves, twigs, and dead branches fell upon them. The yells changed to cries of terror as the natives fled away in the darkness. This meeting with the natives was later spoken of as "the huggery (confusion) at Nauset."

So the human threat to the expedition vanished. But the cold, windy weather continued as they sailed westward along the shore of Cape Cod. Each night they camped on the beach.

As the explorers swung north and east to follow the mainland coast, the scenery changed at last. They could see forested hills, with here and there a creek coming into the ocean, but no harbor big enough for seagoing ships.

One day Clarke surprised them by saying, "Master Jones told me to keep a sharp lookout for a harbor he knows is in this part of the coast."

"How could he know?" they asked.

Clarke shrugged. "I suppose he heard talk from other masters. Or maybe he saw Master John Smith's chart of this coast."

Coppin added, "Jones is right. I know because I've been here before!"

Carver and Bradford spent much time discussing with the others their uncertain future. When they found a site, and the Mayflower brought the settlers to it, would Jones take off for England, leaving them to starve or freeze to death?

Bradford said, "It wouldn't surprise me. I think he has been nice to us recently so he can tell the merchants that he helped us all he could. I don't trust that man."

Carver answered gently. "William, God has brought us this far. We must trust in Him."

December 9 By December 9 the wind had shifted and grown stronger. The shallop was having a difficult time in the open sea. Early darkness and clouds made it impossible to see the shore. At last a big wave hit the rudder, breaking it and tearing the tiller from the helmsman's hand. Before the sail could be hauled down, a mighty blast of wind snapped the mast. Six men grabbed the oars. Forgotten was their search for a harbor; their only aim was to keep the boat from capsizing or smashing on the shore.

Suddenly the wind dropped off and the pull of the waves lessened. An unseen current lifted the boat and carried it toward land in the darkness. The men struggled at the oars but were helpless. In an incredibly short time they found themselves landing on a small island in a sheltered harbor. They were astonished to be alive.

Drenched and nearly frozen stiff but with thanksgiving in their hearts, they climbed out of the boat. After securing the shallop their first concern was to build a fire.

The next day was Sunday. The Pilgrims spent it quietly, resting and drying themselves and their equipment. Two or three repaired the rudder while others spliced the broken mast.

| December 11 |

Early Monday morning, in welcome sunshine and warmer weather, they set out to see the site to which they had been brought by forces beyond their control.

The harbor was well-protected by the contour of the land and large enough to hold several big ships. For two days they carefully observed every aspect of the place, even probing some miles into the woods. They found both level ground and a sizable hill. A river running down into the harbor promised plenty of fresh water. Endless forests would supply fuel for fires, lumber for houses, and good hunting.

Natives had obviously lived here, cleared fields and raised corn, but their village lay in ruins.

Everyone agreed that, since they could not get to northern Virginia, this was where they must settle.

| December 13 |

On Wednesday, December 13, in sunshine and with a favoring wind, they set sail on the return voyage to the Mayflower. Instead of retracing their roundabout route, Clarke and Coppin directed them to sail almost straight south to the tip of Cape Cod. It was not far at all.

While these events were unfolding, the Pilgrims on the Mayflower had trials of their own. The same bad weather had kept them trapped on board ship. More fell sick, and three men had died. Each day the women grew increasingly anxious about their menfolk. Had the boat gone to the bottom in those severe storms? Or had they landed safely only to be attacked and killed by natives?

On the eighth day since the shallop had left the anchorage, the lookout shouted, "Here they come!"

Every able-bodied person hurried onto the deck and crowded against the rail. Eager eyes strained to see loved ones as the shallop winged closer. A sailor in the rigging called out, "I count twelve men on board. They've all come back!"

Alice Mullins pointed to her husband and cried to Priscilla and little Joseph, "There he is! Do you see him?"

"Oh yes! I see him!" Priscilla answered, her eyes shining.

But it was John Alden's face she was looking at, and he was waving at her!

As the explorers scrambled from the shallop onto the Mayflower, families greeted each other with cries of joy and relief. Questions flew back and forth.

"Are you all right? Did you find a place?"

"A wonderful harbor."

"Where?"

"What is it like?"

"A deserted Indian village. Cleared fields."

"Freshwater streams. Level land for houses."

"Huge trees!"

"There's a hill, too. Great for a lookout post. Later we'll have a fort there!" This was Captain Standish's comment as he stood beside Rose.

William Bradford chimed in. "Rich soil, water full of fish, and deer in the forest promise us food aplenty."

Then in a solemn tone he added, "The village seems to have been deserted. Still, there's a chance people might return in the spring and drive us out."

Silence fell on the colonists.

Bradford, standing by Elder Brewster, turned to him said with concern, "Is Dorothy ill? Is that why she did not come on deck to greet us?"

Brewster put an arm around his young lieutenant's shoulder and led him toward the door to the cabins. With a world of understanding in his voice he said, very softly, "William, our Dorothy has left us. She is dead."

He told the stricken husband that his wife had disappeared overboard two days earlier, early on Monday morning. They had searched the shore for miles but found no trace of her. Ocean tides must have taken her body to its final resting place.

Bradford pressed Brewster's hand with both of his. He was unable to say a word before he stumbled to the hatch and descended to the cargo hold. There he would face his tragic loss alone.

No one knows what went through his mind and heart. Apparently he never talked with anyone about this painful experience. In his journal, under the heading "Deaths," he wrote: "December 11, Dorothy, wife to Mr. William Bradford."

People noticed, however, that after the death of his wife Bradford became less quick to judge and criticize others and more caring and understanding.

Brewster returned slowly to the deck, where Jones had joined the crowd.

"So by good luck you found that harbor!" he exclaimed. "Master John Smith marked it on the chart he made of this coast five or six years ago. He called it Plymouth, but you can give it any name you choose."

Elder Brewster told him, "We were led to that place, sir, and we are most thankful. As for the name, the people of old Plymouth were very kind to us. I feel it is appropriate for us to use that name."

Others agreed. Then someone asked Jones, "How soon can we move? Today?"

The master smiled but said they would have to wait for an east wind. Only when the wind was right could they maneuver the ship out of the protective arm of Cape Cod.

| December 16 | On Saturday, December 16, the east wind blew. After thirty-four days at anchor, the Mayflower, led by the shallop, carried the English settlers the last twenty-five miles of their transatlantic voyage. By noon that day the incoming tide brought the vessels to safe anchorage in the harbor John Smith had labeled "Plymouth" on his chart in 1614.

The Brewsters, Bradford, the Carvers, the Hopkins

family, Sam Fuller, Captain and Mrs. Standish, John Alden and Priscilla Mullins and her family, the Billingtons, the Allertons, and others gazed at the wintry scene with mixed feelings.

Some were grateful for the advantages of this site. Others though longingly of the warmer climate of Virginia. They wondered, "Why have things gone wrong for us, that we must settle *here?*"

Chapter 3

Squanto's Astounding Story

For many years before the Mayflower arrived in the New World, the Patuxet tribe had lived by the harbor the Pilgrims would call Plymouth.

The Patuxets were not wanderers. They lived in lodges and made a good living by farming, hunting, and fishing. They were on friendly terms with their neighbors, the Wamponoags, and other nearby tribes.

1614

Once in a while a European ship would visit the coast, but it was not until 1614 that these foreigners made much impression on the natives in the area. Then a new period in history began.

That summer two English ships came into the harbor. Master John Smith—who had earlier been in Jamestown, Virginia—was there to continue charting the eastern coast of America. Thomas Hunt, master of the second ship, was there to get a cargo of dried fish to sell in

Spain. But soon he had a different idea.

Impressed with the physical fitness of the young men as they loaded the dried fish onto his ship, Hunt saw an easy way to make big money for himself when he got to Spain. He would capture the natives and sell them in the slave market at Malaga.

When Master Smith had left to continue mapping the coast, Hunt invited twenty young Patuxet braves to a feast on the ship to celebrate the successful trading. Among them was Tisquantum, or Squanto, one of the most outstanding youths in the village. He was known especially for his speed and endurance in running, and often carried messages from his chief to other tribes. A one-man Postal Service!

The story is that Squanto, who apparently was not married, went to his parents for advice.

"Shall I accept this stranger's invitation?" he asked.

His mother answered quickly, "No! We'll never see you again."

His father thought for a minute and then said, "Yes, my son. It is an honor for you to represent our tribe with these people from another world."

So Squanto was rowed with the other youths out to the ship. In the meantime, Hunt had given secret orders to his first and second mates.

As soon as the braves were seated at the table in the cabin, the doors were quietly closed and locked. The sailors were ordered to raise the anchors and unfurl the sails. Slowly and steadily the ship moved out of Patuxet harbor, heading for Cape Cod.

There was *nothing* Squanto and the others could do.

They had been trained since boyhood never to show fear or anger, so their faces may have been without expression. But this was a harder trial than any had ever faced—even alone in a wintry forest. Yet they showed courage and self-control.

At Nauset on Cape Cod, where the "huggery" between the natives and the Pilgrims would later happen, Hunt stopped to get more water. While there he managed to pick up seven more young natives. They and the Patuxet group were able to talk with each other because most of the tribes in that area spoke different dialects of the same Algonquin language.

During the two or three months they were at sea, the captives probably didn't try to make friends with the English sailors. But they must have picked up quite a bit of English anyway.

After many weary weeks at sea the ship went through the narrow Straits of Gibraltar into the Mediterranean Sea, with Europe on the left side and Africa on the right. The captives who had survived the crossing had no way of knowing they were seeing two different continents at the same time.

Finally the ship came into the harbor of Malaga. The anchors were dropped, ending Squanto's long voyage.

Hunt took his cargo of men to the bustling marketplace and sold them as slaves. Many were taken to North Africa where their lives would be bitter and short. No doubt he congratulated himself on making so much money so easily.

Squanto's fate was different. He was taken as either a slave or servant to a Catholic monastery in Spain. There he lived and worked from the fall of 1614 to about 1616 or 1617. He learned Spanish and may have been taught about the Christian faith.

Then two priests apparently helped him get to England,

where he lived in the London home of a shipping merchant named John Slany. He may have been a servant, or possibly treated like a son.

This was a completely new setting for the Patuxet brave. From the trackless forests of the New World he had now moved to the huge, sprawling, brawling city of London. If he did any running there it was on city streets crowded with people, horses, carriages, and wagons of all kinds.

During the next two years the Patuxet brave became a familiar figure in that part of the city. He was always stared at, pointed at, and talked about with interest and curiosity. At the same time, he was learning a great deal about the English and their language.

1619 By 1619 Squanto became so homesick for his own people and his own forests that Slany, a man with a big heart, arranged to send him home by way of the Nova Scotia fishing fleet.

He told Squanto, "Masters there will help you find a ship that is sailing south along the coast. You can go with them, and they will drop you off at your village."

Slany was right! At the Grand Banks fishing area Squanto met for the second time a man named Thomas Dermer. Dermer had been an officer on Master Smith's ship when it visited Plymouth in 1614. Since then, Dermer had become a master himself, on a different ship.

Squanto told Dermer about Patuxet and its advantages as a trading post for the English. He talked with such enthusiasm that Dermer, instead of sailing southward, took Squanto with him back to England. Squanto must have wondered if he would ever get home again to his people.

When they arrived in England, Dermer introduced Squanto to an Englishman named Sir Ferdinando Gorges. This important man was interested in trading and colonizing and was eager to help his country form strong ties with the natives in New England. He saw that Squanto, because he was able to speak English, could help in building good relationships with the Patuxet and other tribes.

Gorges made plans, supplied money, and sent Master Dermer back to America with Squanto as interpreter, guide, and advisor. In March of 1619 Dermer and Squanto set sail for New England.

They had heard from other sailors about the mysterious epidemic that had struck the natives in New England. An earlier Gorges expedition reported finding one village in ruins, with unburied bones and skulls scattered everywhere.

The Englishmen were not afraid of catching the disease themselves because it had not hurt them noticeably. Squanto probably had no idea whether his tribe had been affected or not.

Finally Dermer's ship reached the harbor at Patuxet. Squanto, eager to see his family, faced a totally unexpected scene. His once-thriving, lively village was in ruins, with no sign of human life anywhere. Lodges were falling to pieces. Fields were overgrown with weeds. It was a place of death.

Even with all his training and experience, Squanto must have been in shock. A lesser man might have gone crazy or killed himself, but not Squanto. Evidently he pulled himself together; the records show that his knowledge and diplomatic skills made it possible, during that summer of 1619, for the English to build new and valuable trading relations with several tribes living along that part of the coast.

Squanto was interested not only in helping the English; even though his own village had been wiped out by disease, he longed to bring honor to the Patuxet tribe of which he was a proud member. The Pilgrim leader Edward Winslow later wrote that the Patuxet brave desired "honor, which he loved as his life and preferred before his peace."[1]

So, as Dermer moved on to another area, Squanto quietly slipped away from the English group to search for surviving Patuxets who might be living in distant villages. While looking for his own people, Squanto seems to have stayed with the nearby Wampanoags. Their chief was called Massassoit.

| 1620 |

Without Squanto at his side, Master Dermer ran into trouble with natives on Long Island and other places. As a result, in 1620, Massassoit captured the Englishman and held him prisoner in the Wampanoag village.

Squanto was there. He told Massassoit, "If you make friends and trade with the English, it will give you a big advantage in dealing with your old enemies, the Narragansetts. You will be stronger than they are!"

The Patuxet brave gave such convincing details of what he had seen and heard in England that finally the chief was convinced. Massassoit set Dermer free to return to his ship and Sir Ferdinando's men.

But Dermer still had not learned how to build good relationships with the different tribes. He kept on making mistakes—and enemies, too.

When Massassoit learned that natives in another area had been killed by Englishmen, the chief blamed Dermer and wanted to take revenge. Then he remembered that the Patuxet brave in Dermer's task force had been Dermer's advisor. Since Massassoit couldn't catch Dermer, he made Squanto his prisoner.

That is how it happened that Squanto was living in the Wampanoag village when the Mayflower and the Pilgrims came into the harbor in December of 1620.

| December 1620 | From the day Master Hunt kidnapped him Squanto's one aim had been to do whatever was necessary, to survive any ordeal, in order to return to his people. For this he had suffered much. He had even crossed the Atlantic a fourth time, only to find his people gone.

What did the future hold for such a man?

1. Edward Winslow, *Good News*, pp. 289-290

Chapter 4

Shocks and Surprises

As soon as the Mayflower dropped anchor in Plymouth harbor, the Pilgrim leaders began mapping the main street of their village. They set land aside for a Common House and other public needs, and outlined plots of suitable size for each family.

Then people drew lots for first choice of plot, second choice, and all the way through the list. Drawing lots was their way of asking God to decide because, for them, no one person or group had the authority to make those decisions. The Pilgrims wanted New Plymouth to have opportunities for all—whether the settler was a Cambridge man like William Brewster, or someone like John Billington, who did not even share their faith. It was a new world, and they turned away from the class privileges that were part of everyday life in England.

During the long months at sea there had been nothing to do. Now dozens of tasks must be done as quickly as possible. Equipment and tools had to be unloaded from the ship.

Trees had to be cut down and, because the settlers did not know about log cabins, sawed into lumber to build their houses. Reeds for roofing had to be gathered.

The men also needed to go hunting and fishing to add to the food supply. Most of the Pilgrims were not very skilled at these tasks; they didn't even have the right kind of fishhooks.

Women and children helped by collecting wood and tending fires, and by cooking whatever food was available. Captain Standish made sure a sentry was standing guard on Lookout Hill every hour of the day and night. The possibility of attack was always in the minds of the Pilgrims.

But it was not the natives who attacked. It was a more deadly enemy: *disease.*

After five months of poor food and crowded living conditions, the Pilgrims—especially the women—were easy victims of a killer disease they called "the sickness."

| Dec./Jan. 1621 |

Six people died in December and eight more in January. So that no one outside the village would know how many had died and how few were left, the survivors buried the bodies at night, in the path between the landing and the village.

| February 1621 |

In February the situation grew worse. Seventeen men, women, and children died during the month. But the remaining Pilgrims didn't give up; they were willing to do whatever needed to be done for the good of the settlement. Even William Bradford, though second in command to Brewster, claimed no special privileges. After doing hard physical labor from

dawn to dark, he shared the unpleasant task of nursing sick and dying men. He also took his turn at sentry duty.

Already the Common House was completed and in use as a hospital and storage place. Two or three family homes were occupied, and others were making good progress.

Such commitment so impressed Master Jones that he remained at Plymouth harbor even after the repairs to the Mayflower were completed. His decision was a happy surprise to the Pilgrims but a shock to the sailors, who were eager to start home because there were no natives around for them to trade and socialize with. The furious sailors threatened to mutiny.

Master Jones paid no attention; he was more concerned about the settlers' needs than the crew's demands. He knew that people still living on board would have no shelter from the bitter weather if the Mayflower left. He was also worried about their lack of food. Several times Jones took a couple of sailors with him and went hunting. They brought back wild ducks and geese, seals, and deer. The sailors wanted to keep all the meat for themselves, but Jones divided it with the colonists. What a change in the gruff captain!

Then one day just as the sun was setting, the settlers were shocked by loud, weird cries coming from the woods beyond Lookout Hill. What they heard was not a battle cry. It sounded like men shouting to cheer each other on. Brewster and Bradford were eager to use this chance to make friendly contact with their unknown neighbors. Standish wanted to fire a cannon shot, just to scare the shouters, but those weapons were still on the ship.

Elder Brewster spoke up. "It is almost dark. I suggest we wait and see what the natives do next."

Standish ordered four men to stand guard around the Common House, slow-matches burning, ready to shoot if necessary. The rest of the men went inside, holding their muskets and expecting a call to action.

In the village and on the Mayflower, the women too were looking and listening anxiously through the long night.

But *nothing happened!*

Dawn came, as peaceful as ever. The Pilgrims went back to work, but they were even more watchful than usual.

That morning Captain Standish had a talk with Master Jones. Later Jones called his crew together. "Men, you are eager to set sail," he said. "Earlier I asked you to help the settlers hoist their cannons out of the hold and take them up the hill and onto the platform prepared for them. You objected, saying that is not the job for which you are paid. Today I am telling you that I will *never* order the anchors raised as long as those cannons are on board. When they are gone, I will give orders to prepare the ship for sailing."

He turned sharply and left them.

The moving of the cannons began that day, with the crew and colonists working together. The hard, slow job took several days. Then the captain fulfilled his promise and ordered a complete overhaul and inspection of all the ship's gear. After being idle for three months, some of the sails and ropes and pulleys needed care and repair.

When the Pilgrims realized that the ship would be leaving before long, they took time to write letters home.

Brewster and Bradford and Edward Winslow wrote detailed reports and suggestions to Robert Cushman, their business agent, and other friends. These would go on the ship when it sailed. (Much of what we know today of the early life of the Pilgrims comes from these letters and journals.)

About this time Captain Standish's house was finished. Rose Standish had died, so he asked John Alden to share the house with him.

"*Thank you*, sir!" the young carpenter answered. "I'll sure be glad to live in a house again, and on shore! I'll help you take care of it, too."

| March 1621 | Several families escaped the sickness unscathed during the hard winter months. During December, January, and February no one died in the Brewster, Mullins, Hopkins, and Billington families. Then in March William Mullins fell sick and died, followed by his wife and small son.

In his journal Bradford wrote: "Of the some 100 persons who came on the Mayflower, scarce 50 remain. And of these, in the time of greatest distress, there was but some six or seven healthy persons."[1]

The Brewsters welcomed Priscilla Mullins into their family and home. She was worn out by nursing her parents and little brother, and numbed by her loss. Now John Alden was able to see her more frequently and to help comfort her. They made plans to marry.

Elizabeth Tilley was another young girl who had lost both parents to the sickness. Governor and Mrs. Carver took her into their home. Everyone was cared for in Plymouth.

Signs of spring were beginning to appear, marking the end of the terrible winter. Soon it would be time for the settlers to sow wheat, oats, and barley. They had brought barrels of these grains for planting, but with all the delays they had been forced to eat most of these supplies. They still had the corn they had found on Cape Cod, but they had no idea how to plant or cook it. They might yet go hungry—or starve to death.

Captain Standish feared that with the improving weather would come the natives who had lived in the village. He thought they might return to claim their lands. Knowing how unprotected the community was, he gathered the few healthy men in the Common House. He said to them, "It is important now for you to learn military orders. That means: *what to do if we are attacked*. We are few; each man must know his responsibilities."

While they were studying and learning those rules, the thing they had most feared happened.

A shot rang out from Lookout Hill. As the men rushed to the street the sentry screamed: *"Indians! Indians coming!"*

Captain Standish barked an order and the men formed a line. Soon they saw one lone native. The smiling man carried no weapons.

Pointing at himself, the man said, "Samoset! Samoset!"

Then he waved at the settlers. "Ingliss?" he asked. "Ingliss? Samoset . . . know . . . Ingliss . . . sailors."

His openness took the settlers by surprise. While Carver and Brewster tried to talk with him, Standish and the other men kept looking suspiciously in all directions. This fellow

could be a decoy, they thought.

They could hardly understand a word Samoset said, but when he pretended to drink from a bottle, they understood what he wanted. They gave him "strong water and biscuits, and cheese, and pudding, with a piece of duck, all of which he liked well."[2] When he had finished eating, the conversation continued.

The still-wary settlers learned that Samoset was from a northern Algonquin tribe living on the Pemaquid River. He was visiting the Wampanoags, and he seemed to want to make friends. However, they could hardly understand him because most of his English words were those used in trading. After a while Samoset gave up and prepared to leave. Then he said, "Samoset go Massassoit. Squanto spik mush Ingliss."

The Pilgrims had no idea what Samoset was trying to tell them. As he left the village, several men, still holding muskets, walked with him as far as the thick woods.

A few days later, with work going on as usual in the village, another shot from Lookout Hill alerted the people.

Once more the women called the children indoors; the men dropped their tools and grabbed guns, lighting the slow-matches as quickly as they could.

A tall, thin native came into view carrying a bow and some arrows. It was not Samoset but an older man with a serious, sad face.

Someone suggested shooting him. Standish growled, "Hold your fire! He has done us no harm." His cool-headed command may well have kept Plymouth Colony from coming to a quick, bloody end.

The warrior held up one arm in solemn salute.

"Welcome, brothers," he said. "Samoset say you needs help. Me, Squanto. I helps you?"

Mouths dropped open and muskets were lowered.

Women and children came close and listened too. Sorrow gripped their hearts as they heard Squanto's story of being stolen from his village. When he told about coming home with Master Dermer and finding his family and tribe dead and the village in ruins, tears were in many eyes.

Squanto went on. "When I hear white mens in Patuxet dying I no care. Samoset tell me, "Families—women and babies! If Squanto no help, all die. Samoset talk long and wise to Chief Massassoit. Chief gave me free to come see."

Squanto's face softened as he looked at the children gathered around. "I like see little ones in my village again! I stay? I helps you?"

"Oh, please stay!" someone cried out. The tall brave was surrounded by welcoming smiles.

Squanto had found a new tribe. And when Stephen and Elizabeth Hopkins and their children took him into their home and hearts, he also had a new family to love. He felt needed and honored.

Finding food was the community's greatest immediate need. One of the first things Squanto did was to show Giles Hopkins and other boys how to go barefoot into the mud flats at low tide and squash out eels, grabbing them and stuffing them into bags.

"This is easy! And fun!" they shouted.

It was also good meat, and plenty of it.

The waters were full of fish. Squanto introduced the settlers to the many ways of catching different kinds of fish in rivers and the sea.

"No go hungry," he told them, shaking his head. "Plenty fish."

One person who watched with special interest what Squanto was doing for the colony was Master Jones. He smiled. The settlers were in good hands. It would be all right for him to leave. He gave orders for casks to be filled with fresh water and other supplies loaded onto the ship.

When the Mayflower was ready, Jones had another surprise for the settlers.

"Friends," he said, "there are empty living quarters on the Mayflower. Any of you who would like to go with me are welcome to do so. I will not charge you a single penny!"

What an easy way to escape from all the dangers, difficulties, and uncertainty of life in the New World! But not one Pilgrim, not one Adventurer accepted Jones' kind offer.

Instead they asked him, "How long will it take for you to get to England?"

Jones shrugged. "That depends on the weather and the ship. Maybe six weeks, two months. Maybe more."

The Pilgrims hated to see the ship leave. It had been their home, their center of activity, and their source of security for nearly eight months. And Jones, who at first had disliked the Separatists and criticized them, had undergone a complete change of heart. He'd stayed with them even when the crew rebelled, giving people shelter and providing food. They tried to express their appreciation and their fears for the ship's safety.

He tried to encourage them. "Don't worry, friends! I'm sure we'll get safely to England. And as soon as I can settle my affairs, I'll get on the next ship heading this way, and make my home here with all of you!"

What a surprise! He had become one of them.

Toward the end of March, on a clear day with a favoring wind, the anchors were hauled up and the Mayflower set sail. The whole company gathered on Lookout Hill to watch. Near the four Brewsters, John Alden stood beside Priscilla Mullins, quietly holding her hand so she would not feel alone.

Squanto was with the Hopkins family, adding his strength to them and to all the settlers.

On the hill a cannon fired a farewell salute. It was answered by one from the Mayflower.

Of the 102 people who had sailed from old Plymouth, forty-eight had died. That left twenty-five men, twenty-five children and teenagers, and four married women. Their thoughts were centered on the battered ship as it left the harbor and slowly disappeared.

They were worried, and no wonder. The Mayflower carried all their letters and reports. If the ship should run into trouble and go to the bottom of the Atlantic, no one in England, Holland, or northern Virginia would ever know what had happened to the settlers. People would think the Mayflower had sunk with all on board. Who would guess that fifty-four people were stranded in New

England, hoping for help from home?

For the colony to grow and be permanent it would need more people. More animals were needed too—more cows, sheep, pigs, and chickens—as well as cloth for new clothes and leather for shoes.

If the Mayflower sank there would be no way the settlers could contact people at home. All they could do then would be to hope some English ship just happened to come into the harbor. They felt absolutely helpless.

Perhaps Elder Brewster was the only person whose faith in their settlement never wavered. When others were worried and doubtful, he said to them, "Look hard, and see them coming—two sails—three. Then mark you in how short a time there come fleets of sail to us, with kith and kin."[3]

They looked, but saw no sails. They could only hope and pray.

1. William Bradford, *Plymouth Plantation,* pp. 61-63.

2. John C. Miller, *The First Frontier,* p. 35

3. Quoted by Ernest Gebler, *The Plymouth Adventure*, p. 366

Chapter 5

Joy and Tears

Next morning the harbor looked very bare and deserted. Only the open shallop rode at anchor. The settlers asked each other, "If the Mayflower has a smooth crossing, how soon can we expect a ship from home to come sailing in?"

One hopeful person answered, "Maybe in October, or November."

"That's impossible!" another settler exclaimed. "Our friends and agents in England will have to contact people in Holland and make plans. That'll take a lot of time. My guess is that the relief ship cannot arrive until next spring or summer."

That was a long time to wait, not knowing if people would ever come.

In the meantime, with Squanto's guidance and help, the men and boys were busy preparing the old Patuxet fields for a new crop of corn. It was hard labor, with no horse to pull a plow. He taught them to not scatter the kernels as

they would grains of wheat but to plant them in rows of little hills. In each hill they put three kernels of corn and some shad or other fish for fertilizer.

The women learned to grind the dried kernels for cornmeal and to use it instead of wheat flour for bread and other foods.

From the Wampanoag village Squanto brought a supply of pumpkin seeds. The English were familiar with this vegetable, which would remain good all winter. They were glad to add another crop to their gardens.

Other times Squanto led the men into the forests and taught them how to stalk deer and wild birds. Squanto used his bow and arrows, but the settlers had only their noisy firearms.

There must have been excitement in the village when Squanto and the Pilgrim hunters first carried home wild turkeys.

"Look!" boys yelled. "Turkeys! Big as three roosters!"

The fear of starvation was gone.

That spring Squanto helped the colony in another way which was just as important as providing food. He was an ambassador for them in building a good, lasting relationship with Chief Massassoit and the Wampanoag warriors.

When the chief and his braves paid a formal visit to Plymouth, Squanto was their interpreter. He translated between the two languages and helped the English and the Native Americans understand each other's customs and values. With Squanto's help they signed a formal treaty, promising to respect and deal honestly with each other. They agreed to give mutual support in case the Wampanoags were attacked by their traditional enemies, the Naragansetts, or if any hostile tribe threatened Plymouth.

Summer 1621 Spring turned to summer and the sickness was gone. The people were no longer skin and bones, and their fields and gardens were growing well. The happy voices of children sounded up and down the village street where houses looked more like home every day.

Married now, Priscilla Mullins and John Alden were living in the Mullins' house. John was putting finishing touches to it while Priscilla enjoyed finding places for her family possessions.

From time to time the settlers faced internal problems. John Billington would often break some rule of the colony, but the organization created by the Compact was able to deal with each difficult situation.

During the summer, Governor Carver, who was over 60, died of a stroke while working in the fields. That was a blow to the colony.

William Bradford was elected governor in his place, a position he held with honor for many years. Democracy was beginning to work in a small way and to prove its value.

During all these weeks and months the settlers had many moments of fear and doubt.

"Has the Mayflower reached England?" they wondered. "If not, what will become of us and our children?"

Young Governor Bradford helped them to see that Squanto's presence should give them hope. He told them Squanto had been sent by God to help them survive that first winter. They should have no fear, he said.

By this time a different question bothered some families. If help came, would the colony be forced to move to Virginia, where they had permission to settle? They had grown to love this place and they didn't want to move.

Most kept quiet about their fears, but Billington never tried to hide his feelings. "We are in the wrong place," he complained, "and it is all Brewster's fault. He should have made Jones take us to northern Virginia. Then people in England would know where to look for us. As it is, if that wreck of a Mayflower goes down, we are sunk too."

October came, bringing gorgeous colors on the trees and even bigger crops than expected. They would have more than enough food to last through the winter. The settlers looked at each other and their snug little village with amazement and joy. Their future was still uncertain, but their hearts overflowed with gratitude for all they had received and accomplished.

"Let's celebrate!" they said. "Let's have a party! A harvest feast, all of us together!"

The idea caught on.

"Oh yes," someone said, "and let's invite Chief Massassoit. To show our thanks for the help he and Squanto have given us."

November, 1621 Soon Squanto and a group of men went to the village to invite the chief and some of his braves for a feast of thanksgiving. They returned to Plymouth with startling news. There was *nothing* the Wampanoags enjoyed as much as a feast. They would *all* come!

A day was decided upon and plans were made for the big party. Men and boys went hunting and fishing. John Alden made extra tables to hold the food by building sawhorses and laying planks on them. Women and girls baked cornbread and cooked vegetables.

They also made pies that were filled with sweetened pumpkin. The Pilgrims were accustomed to eating meat pies as a main course. The women didn't know if the men would like pies for dessert, but they made quite a few of them anyway. They also directed the roasting of meat over big outdoor fires.

When Chief Massassoit and his people came out of the forest they were given a great welcome. Native Americans and English families began eating together and making friends, even if they couldn't understand each others' words.

It was a day full of laughter and fun and appreciation. They probably sang for each other too, and maybe the Wampanoags demonstrated their native dances.

The party went on for three days. The pumpkin pies didn't last nearly so long; they were delicious and disappeared quickly.

The rest of October passed quickly as the settlers

restored order to the village. The shorter days and colder nights told them winter was coming. And with it came doubts and fears, creeping again into the minds of many settlers.

"How long can we live here?" they wondered. "What kind of life will it be for our children if help never comes?"

November 9, 1621 It was on November 9, 1621, that a warning shot sounded from Lookout Hill.

"What now?" the settlers asked. They went outdoors and looked toward the forest. Was it an enemy attack?

Then they saw the sentry, jumping up and down, pointing out to sea and yelling at the top of his voice.

"A ship! There's a ship coming!"

Excitement raced through the settlement. People dropped what they were doing and rushed to the shore.

"Hallelujah!" they shouted. "Friends from home!"

Then Captain Standish roared a command. "Wait! It could be enemies. A Spanish or a French warship."

He signaled the men to fall into line.

Shocked into silence, the settlers waited almost without breathing as the ship slowly came closer.

At last they saw their beloved English flag flying from the masthead. Shouts shattered the stillness. People went almost crazy with joy and relief.

The good ship Fortune came into harbor exactly one year after the Mayflower reached Cape Cod. That welcome ship was bringing friends, families, and a future to the Plymouth colony.

Sails were furled and anchors splashed into the water. Soon people began coming ashore. There was complete confusion and joy as passengers and settlers greeted one another. Everyone was talking at once, and tears of gratitude were on many faces.

William and Mary Brewster, and their sons Love and Wrastle, hugged and kissed the teenagers they had left in Holland. Other families were reunited too, and new families were welcomed with open arms and deep thanksgiving.

At last the Mayflower survivors knew that Master Jones and the Mayflower had made it safely to London.

Their business agent, Robert Cushman, had come on the Fortune too. "That's right," he said. "Jones reached London on May 6, after an easy trip of scarcely seven weeks."

"Then why didn't he come back with you?"

"There wasn't time. After giving a full report to the other owners of the ship, he had his own affairs to settle. He will come when he can." Cushman said he would go back on the Fortune when the return cargo had been loaded.

Then Brewster and Bradford asked the question they all feared. "Do we have to move to Virginia?"

"No indeed!" Cushman said. "On June first I got your patent changed. You are now the Plymouth Company, with permission to settle in this area."

Later he told them privately that the new patent was made out in the name of "John Pierce and his associates" to avoid drawing attention to Elder Brewster, who was still wanted by English authorities.

For a while most of the passengers spent their nights on the Fortune. The young Brewsters stayed with their parents in the village.

John and Priscilla also shared their home with another family. They were already beginning to fulfill the goal of Priscilla's parents, who had dreamed of being important members of the colony. Together they had many children and lived long lives. Priscilla was 80 when she died, and John lived to 87.

Plymouth became a beehive of activity. There was work for everybody, with the Mayflower families showing the new folks what to do. Once more the men went into the forest with axes and saws to get materials for new houses.

After a few days Elder Brewster and Governor Bradford gathered new settlers and old in the Common House, which was no longer a hospital. They wanted to welcome the new residents formally, share with them the triumphs and tragedies of the Mayflower voyage, and explain how they came to settle where they did instead of in Virginia. Everyone was present, including Squanto.

Elder Brewster stood up, his face glowing as he looked ever the large Plymouth family. His first words gave heartfelt thanks for Master Jones' safe and speedy trip home. Then he thanked the new settlers for their readiness to come to the New World so soon after the return of the Mayflower. Then he turned the meeting over to the Pilgrims.

Different people spoke of the dangers and difficulties the

Mayflower group had faced. They mentioned the delays and the loss of the use of the Speedwell. They told of running into the autumn storms that had forced them north, away from Virginia. Others recalled the seeming miracles that had saved them, such as having the house-screw available when it was needed to repair the broken beam in the main cabin of the Mayflower.

With tears they spoke of the sickness and the loss of many dear ones. They gave thanks for the new settlers who had dared to come and join the colony.

They told of the expedition in the shallop and of how the men were saved when the crippled boat was lifted by wind and tide and brought to safety in this harbor, to this ideal location for their colony.

They remembered Master Jones' change of heart and how he had stayed with them and helped them. They did not know until much later that Jones would never fulfill his plan to return and live in Plymouth. Before his affairs were settled he fell sick and died.

Finally Elder Brewster stood up again and looked around the crowded room. Then in a strong, warm voice he told of how Squanto had come to their rescue at exactly the right moment. He told of the things the Patuxet brave had done to keep them from starving to death, and of how he was an important link in building good trade relations between the growing colony and nearby tribes.

The settlers echoed the elder's words and feelings. Squanto understood that he was loved, respected, and honored. It was a happy moment; there was nothing in it to hint that Squanto's time with the English settlers might be coming to an end.

That winter and the following spring the Plymouth colony flourished. Not only did the settlers satisfy their needs for food and clothing; they also collected and stored furs and other valuable trade goods to send back to London on the next ship.

But one piece of unfinished business still worried Brewster and Bradford. They were honest men, yet in 1620 they had stolen ten bushels of corn from the native farmers on Cape Cod. They had intended to pay for the corn but had never done so. Because of the stolen corn, the native farmers distrusted and feared the settlers.

| September 1622 | So in 1622 the colony leaders decided to go to Cape Cod to repay their debt. Getting there in the shallop would be easy, but now could they contact natives who always ran away when they saw the settlers?

The answer to that question was simple: "Squanto will help us!"

| October 1622 | Squanto liked the idea. He enjoyed the sense of power he felt when he could bring people together.

A small group set out, with Governor Bradford as their leader. They came quickly to Cape Cod.

There Squanto again proved his worth as an ambassador. He contacted the local farmers and told them the English had come to pay for their corn. The farmers were pleased, and relieved to learn they had nothing to fear from these strangers.

The news of this payment spread quickly and natives gathered by the dozens. It was a great occasion.

English money had no value to the native people of Cape Cod. Instead, the settlers opened boxes and gave the natives things they could not make or find in the New World—woven cloth of bright colors and steel knives and other tools. Small mirrors seemed like magic to them, and they loved jewelry and trinkets.

November 1622 But then tragedy struck. Bradford wrote later that while the Plymouth men were still on Cape Cod, "Squanto fell sick of an Indian fever, bleeding much at the nose (which the Indians take for a symptom of death) and within a few days he died there."[1]

This was a terrible shock for Bradford and the others. They could hardly believe it. Squanto, their friend for eighteen months—Squanto, to whom they owed their lives and the healthy growth of their colony—Squanto was dead?

The shallop returned at once to Plymouth. It was a sad homecoming for the settlers, bearing as they did the news of their loss—and probably Squanto's body, bringing it back to his home village for traditional ceremonies.

It was a sudden and painful end to a heartwarming relationship between Squanto and the Mayflower Pilgrims. The Patuxet diplomat had saved the English families, and in caring for them he had found a family and a new tribe to live for.

The people of Plymouth never forgot their Patuxet friend. Even now, almost 400 years later, Squanto is remembered and honored. Without his help, the story of the Pilgrims might have ended in a very different way, and America today would be a very different place.

1. William Bradford, *Plymouth Plantation*, p. 114

It Was No Accident

Was the Plymouth Colony a mistake? Some people think so, because the Pilgrims had planned to build their community in northern Virginia. Where they actually did settle was many miles north of their destination.

William Brewster, a deeply religious man, didn't think any part of the Pilgrims' story happened by accident. When someone suggested that building the colony in Plymouth was a mistake, the Pilgrim leader would agree that the location was not the place where the Pilgrims had planned to make their settlement. But Brewster would argue that they were Divinely directed to Plymouth.

He had many reasons why he felt the site of the Plymouth Colony was an ideal location. Where else in three thousand miles of New World coastline, he would ask, could the Pilgrims have found:

- a deserted village in which to build their homes?
- corn fields ready for their plows?

85

- rich forests to give them lumber for houses, fuel for fires, and plenty of game?
- a river and a harbor full of fish?

And where else could they have found a man like Squanto? he would ask. If not for Squanto's help, perhaps none of the Mayflower Pilgrims would have survived to welcome the Fortune.

"So, you see," Brewster would say, "New Plymouth is the right place for us!"

Glossary

Adventurers: people who joined the Mayflower Pilgrims hoping to find riches in the New World rather than for religious reasons

allegiance: loyalty

ambush: hiding to make a surprise attack

appendix: a part of the large intestine

bristling: short, stiff hair

cooper: a carpenter who makes barrels

covenant (verb): to promise or pledge

decoy: something leading to a trap

democracy: government by the people, through representatives or directly

diplomat: one wise in dealing with other groups

eel: a fish with a snake-like body

elder: a church leader who is not a member of the clergy

flash-pan: part of a musket, a small pan used to hold a charge of gunpowder. This charge, when ignited by the slow-match, ignites the musket's main charge.

flint and steel: a type of stone and a piece of metal which produce sparks when struck together; used before matches to start a fire

helmsman: a person who steers a ship

hold: the interior of a ship below the deck

hospitable: friendly, welcoming

huggery: old-fashioned word for confusion or a puzzle

keel: the principal structural support of a ship that runs along the center of the bottom from stem to stern

leeboards: flat boards lowered into the water to lessen a boat's downwind drift

longboat: the longest boat carried by a sailing ship

master: the captain of a ship

meet: old-fashioned word for "suitable"

musket: a gun fired from the shoulder

navigation: the skill of directing a ship's course

opium: a drug made from a type of poppy

patent: a document granting a right or privilege

pilgrim: a wanderer, often one with a special goal or destination

point-blank: directly, without question

purser: the ship's officer in charge of money matters

rigging: chains, ropes, etc. used for controlling sails or holding a ship's masts in place

rudder: a steering device on a ship

seamanship: skill in sailing a ship

seaworthy: in good condition; suitable for use at sea

Separatists: people who left the king's church for religious reasons

shallop: a small open boat, with sail and oars

sick bay: a ship's hospital

slow-match: a long-burning wick, used to ignite the powder in a musket's flash-pan

subscribe: to sign a document as a way of showing consent or support

tiller: a handle for turning a ship's rudder

The Mayflower Passengers
by Family Groups

John Alden (1)

Isaac Allerton (6)
wife: Mary
son: Bartholomew
daughters: Mary, Remember
servant (boy): John Hooke

John Allerton (1)

John Billington (4)
wife: Ellen
sons: Francis, John

William Bradford (2)
wife: Dorothy

William Brewster (6)
wife: Mary
sons: Love, Wrastle
servants (boys): Richard Moore, (name unknown) Moore

Richard Britteridge (1)

Peter Browne (1)

John Carver (8)
wife: Catherine
young woman in their care: Desire Minter
servants: John Howland, Roger Wilder; servants (boys): William Latham, Jasper More; a maid-servant (name unknown)

James Chilton (3)
wife: (name unknown)
daughter: Mary

Richard Clarke (1)

Francis Cooke (2)
son: John

John Crackston (2)
son: John

Francis Eaton (3)
wife: Sarah
son: Samuel

Thomas English (1)

Moses Fletcher (1)

Edward Fuller (3)
wife: Ann
son: Samuel

Samuel Fuller (2)
servant: William Butten (died at sea)

Richard Gardiner (1)

John Goodman (1)

Stephen Hopkins (8)
wife: Elizabeth
sons: Giles, Damaris, Oceanus (born at sea)
daughter: Constance
servants: Edward Dotey, Edward Leister

Edmund Margeson (1)

Christopher Martin (4)
wife: (name unknown)
servants: Solomon Prower, John Langemore

William Mullins (5)
wife: Alice
son: Joseph
daughter: Priscilla
servant: Robert Carter

Degory Priest (1)

John Ridgdale (2)
  wife: Alice

Thomas Rogers (2)
  son: Joseph

Miles Standish (2)
  wife: Rose

Edward Tilley (4)
  wife: Anne
  children under their care (cousins): Humility Cooper,
  Henry Samson

John Tilley (3)
  wife: Bridget
  daughter: Elizabeth

Thomas Tinker (3)
  wife: (name unknown)
  son: (name unknown)

John Turner (3)
  sons: (2; names unknown)

Richard Warren (1)

William White (6)
  wife: Susanna
  son: Peregrine (born at sea)
  daughter: Resolved
  servants: William Holbeck, Edward Thompson

Thomas Williams (1)

Edward Winslow (5)
  wife: Elizabeth
  child under their care: Ellen Moore (Richard Moore's sister)
  servants: George Soule, Elias Story

Gilbert Winslow (1) (Edward Winslow's brother)

References and Resources

References Used by Author

Charlton, W. *The Second Mayflower Adventure*. (Boston, 1957)

Gebler, Ernest. *The Plymouth Adventure*. (New York, 1950)

Lord, Arthur. *Plymouth and the Pilgrims*.

Marshall, Peter and David Manuel. *The Light and the Glory*. (Old Tappan, NJ, 1977)

Salisbury, Neal. *"Squanto: Last of the Patuxets"* in *Struggle and Survival in Colonial America*. Edited by David G. Swet and Gary B. Nash. (Berkeley, CA, 1981)

Starr, M. *"Thanksgiving."* in *Evangelical Beacon*. (Nov. 6, 1989)

Vrooman, Lee. *The Faith that Built America*. (New York, 1955)

Willison, George F. *Saints and Strangers*. (New York, 1946)

Original Sources

Bradford, William. *Of Plymouth Plantation* 1620-1647. Edited by W.C.Ford (Massachusetts, 1912). Edited by S. E. Morison (New York, 1959).

Bradford, William, and Edward Winslow. *Mourt's Relations*. (1622)

Robinson, John. *Collected Works*. (London, 1851)

Smith, John. *Description of New England*. (1616)

Winslow, Edward. *Hypocrisy Unmasked*. (London,1646)

_____. *Good Newes from New England*. (London, 1623)

Other Sources

Arber, Edward. *Story of the Pilgrim Fathers* 1606-1623. (Boston, 1897)

Benet, Stephen Vincent. *Western Star.*

Cushman, Robert. *Sermons, Tracts, Letters.*

Hackney, Noel C. L. *Mayflower: Classic Ships No. 2* (London, 1970)

Massachusetts Historical Collections

Miller, John C. *The First Frontier: Life in Colonial America* (New York, 1966)

Morton, Nathaniel. *New Englands Memoriall.* (Cambridge, 1669; reprint Boston, 1903)

Pilkington, Roger. *I Sailed on the Mayflower. (1990)*

Pulsifer. *Plymouth Colony Records.* (Boston, 1861)

Smith, Bradford. *Bradford of Plymouth.*

Wyndham, Lee. *Thanksgiving. (New York, 1963)*

More Good Reading From Harbinger House

Mystery on Mackinac Island
by Anna W. Hale

One summer day rental bicycles start disappearing all over the island. Hunter, an Ottawa boy whose grandfather taught him how to track animals, is certain that he, with the help of his new tourist friends, can find the culprit.

"Hale utilizes her setting effectively, giving young readers a feel for historic and atmospheric Mackinac Island, and she supplies plenty of action."—School Library Journal

184 pages. 6 × 8. Ages 8-12   ISBN 0-943173-34-5 Paper $9.95

The Very First Thanksgiving:
Pioneers on the Rio Grande by Bea Bragg

Twenty three years before the Pilgrims arrived at Plymouth a great thanksgiving feast was held along the Rio Grande. The adventures of two young brothers and their pet goat on the expedition led by Don Juan de Oñate, tell the story. Beautifully illustrated by Antonio Castro.

"Bea Bragg has ingeniously wrapped authentic history in a palatable story that will delight a youngster with its adventure and humor".— Martha Peters, El Paso Times

64 pages. 7¼ × 8¾. Ages 7-12   ISBN 0-943173-22-1 Paper $7.95

The Streets are Paved with Gold
by Fran Weissenberg

Fourteen-year-old Debbie Gold, daughter of Russian-Jewish immigrants, finds herself caught between family traditions and the new world of friends and interests she is just discovering.

"Debbie's first-person narration lends immediacy and emotion to her experiences. The integrity and generosity of the Gold family will impress readers young and old."—Publishers Weekly

160 pages. 5⅜ × 8. Ages 12 and up   ISBN 0-943173-51-5 Paper $6.95

To order, contact your favorite bookseller or distributor.

· Harbinger House ·

BOOKS OF INTEGRITY

TUCSON

About the Author and Illustrator

 natural storyteller, who has "always loved history", ANNA W. HALE was born in New York City. Later her family moved to New Jersey, where she was raised in a house that played a role in Washington's Battle of Princeton. After graduation from Wells College she became a professional governess and helped to raise 35 children in many areas of the United States and Europe. Her popular book for children, *Mystery on Mackinac Island,* was published by Harbinger House in her retirement years. Now living in Tucson, she still loves to dress up as a Pilgrim and tell the Thanksgiving story to children and adults.

 ARIA HAZEN-VORIS is a free-lance illustrator who earned her B.A. in Graphic Design from Northern Arizona University. She recently returned to her native city of Tucson after spending four years exploring other parts of the country, including Alaska, where she met her artist husband, Jack.